Life is Love

Innovation

Freedom

Epiphanies

Life is love's omniscient vigor energizing

innovative inspirations expanding my

financial freedom eulogizing my

epiphanies turning the world

in audacious acumen as I walk-n-wisdom

unattached to life situations...

Robert Wilson

Editing by Amy Lignor

May_____

life flow in the lavish avalanche of
copious copiousness, now to eternity, in
the right way, in a loving way, under
grace in a Divine blessed way, and in
Divine order...**NOW**!

ISBN: 1938634144
ISBN-13: 978-1-938634-14-7

Life is Love Innovation

Freedom Epiphanies

by Cowboy Wisdom Visionary Vitality

Eulogizes my Broadway Brilliance unsheathing my Rainbow Realness to showcase my esteemed enterprising wise; to open the world to state-of-the-art entrepreneurialism because I opened my eyes to see my talent to dance in my dreams, daring me to dawn revolutionary, emancipating astuteness which magnetized my cascading cash flow now to eternity in a loving, blessed way...

Life is Love Innovation Freedom Epiphanies is dedicated to my friend Bea Pourier Fisher Fortune…

Carolyn Dawn Good is the cover artist. She is a gifted cross-disciplinary artist who is skilled at custom transformational painting. Her blog is: www.rhiah.tumblr.com.

Thank you for purchasing Life is Love Innovation Freedom Epiphanies

Life * Love* Innovation * Freedom
*<u>Epiphanies</u>!

I Am The Sprightly Light of My Hearts Delight

I Applaud My Divine Deity

I Am Omnific Terrific, Savoring Sassy, Sumptuous Success!

I Am a Spiritual 'Seer' Energizing My Omniscient Omnificence!

Divine Light

Broadway Brilliant

Animated Adroit Wit

My Tangy Sprightliness Zeniths My Inspiring Clarity

My Spiritual Star Unsheathes My Worldly Wisdom

My Mind Is Clear and My Visions Are Pure

Wisdom Illuminations

Electrifying Oomph

Golden New Way

I Am Sunrise Wise Revealing My Sunset Supremacy

My Heart's Delight

Rainbow Realness

My Colorful Charisma

Immaculate Imagination

My Mind Is Clear and My Visions Are Pure

My Visionary Sage

LIFE IS LOVE INNOVATION FREEDOM
EPIPHANIES

By Robert A. Wilson

For more books like this one, visit Robert A.
Wilson's website at:
http://cowboy-wisdom.com/

Printed in the United States of America
The publisher offers discounts on this book when
ordered in bulk quantities. For more information,
contact Sales Department, Phone 815-290-9605,
Email:
sales@FreedomOfSpeechPublishing.com

Freedom of Speech Publishing, Leawood KS,
66224
www.FreedomOfSpeechPublishing.com
ISBN: 1938634144
ISBN-13: 978-1-938634-14-7

A SPECIAL THANK YOU TO YOU!

On behalf of everyone at Freedom Of Speech Publishing, thank you for choosing Life is Love Innovation Freedom Epiphanies for your reading enjoyment.

As an added bonus and special thank you, for purchasing Life is Love Innovation Freedom Epiphanies, you can enjoy discounts and special promotions on other Freedom of Speech Publishing products. Visit www.freedomeofspeech.com/vip to learn more.

We are committed to providing you with the highest level of customer satisfaction possible. If for any reason you have questions or comments, we are delighted to hear from you. Email us at cs@freedomofspeechpublishing.com or visit our website at:
http://freedomofspeechpublishing.com/contact-us-2/.

If you enjoyed Life is Love Innovation Freedom Epiphanies, visit www.freedomofspeechpublishing.com for a list of similar books or upcoming books.

Again, thank you for your patronage. We look forward to providing you more entertainment in the future.

Acknowledgements

A heartfelt thanks to my Mom and Dad who have passed for being my parents and the work ethic and moral values they instilled in me. I understand I wasn't always the easiest child…

I thank my family and extended family: Nieces, Nephews, Aunts, Uncles, Cousins, Sisters and Brothers for being a part of my life.

I thank every one of my friends for being a part of my life.

I thank Amy Lignor (www.thewritecompanion.com): published author, editor, ghostwriter, reviewer, and a truly dynamic writer.

I thank God, Mrs. Universe, the womb of unconditional love and enterprising energies, all people, spiritual ethers, metaphysical realms, physical playgrounds, mystical magical heavens of miracles, and all realized and unrealized sources in the cosmos, for opening the way to authorize and allow me to experience my life, *my way*.

I thank all my listeners and guests on *Cowboy Wisdom NLI Radio* at: www.blogtalkradio.com/cwbywsdm.

I am thankful for Patrick Kungle and Girard Sagmiller with *Freedom of Speech Publishing* for all they do for me.

I thank everybody who buys and reads in order to expand their lives in a perfect way.

I am thankful for my life everyday and in every way, under grace in a perfect way.

I love life and life loves me!

Contents

Preface.. xii

Life * Love * Innovation* Freedom Epiphanies........1

I Am The Sprightly Light of My Hearts Delight 6

I Applaud My Divine Deity 9

I Am Omnific Terrific, Savoring Sassy, Sumptuous Success! 11

I Am a Spiritual 'Seer' Energizing My Omniscient Omnificence! 15

Divine Light 19

Broadway Brilliant 24

Animated Adroit Wit 29

My Tangy Sprightliness Zeniths My Inspiring Clarity 31

My Spiritual Star Unsheathes My Worldly Wisdom 34

My Mind Is Clear and My Visions Are Pure 36

Wisdom Illuminations...38

Electrifying Oomph..39

I Am Sunrise Wise Revealing My Sunset Supremacy
.... 44

My Heart's Delight 47

Rainbow Realness 50

Immaculate Imagination 60

My Mind Is Clear and My Visions Are Pure............ 67

My Visionary Sage.. 69

A SPECIAL THANK YOU TO YOU!.................. 74

Preface

This vision is written in first person, so when you read this read it as if you, yourself, wrote it.

I allow the words to expand me as I read the book. Then I choose to listen my daily escapades. For my highest outcome read out loud. Life is Love Innovation Freedom Epiphanies is written in the first person so as I read this I realize I am reading as I written the subliminal messages of expanding wisdom. To opening my eyes to a crisp new collaborating energy that opens my heart eulogies to sing a trendsetting song of success...

I now understand the essence of love is letting out venomous figures expanding into love is life's omniscient vigor expanding my wisdom to allow the world turn in wisdom as I walk-n-wisdom...

Life is love innovation freedom epiphanies mirrors my friend Bea in the way she enjoyed life and lived life her way. As I now admit to all the people that crossed the river before me left me with guts to write books to understand the aggrandizing awesomeness of life because they all allowed me to grow up my way without judgment...

As the readers reads Life is Love Innovation Freedom Epiphanies please allow the words open up your visions. As the reader reads this book listen in your daily life to see how the reader now hears the words in your daily life.

Thank You to all the readers and people that I have and will encounter in my life now to eternity...

Life * Love * Innovation* Freedom
Epiphanies

Cowboy Wisdom Visionary Vitality

Thus, I begin…

My eyes see the glory in my life, in flawless sunlight of dawning love, innovation, freedom epiphanies that effortlessly expand my roadrunner rebellious wit…

Unlatches and releases my dimwitted devious coyote coyness by dispatching all attachment to thinking I had a past. Because in the old days we did whatever…

Because I had to always be spouting my doubt by bellowing my whiny wimpy 'know it all' palaver pitifully thinking I was somebody important in egotistical sliminess…

Clanking my coyote cowardice and draining me in a peevish mustiness because I was swirling in my smell, in the tell that reeks with insecurity and opens my eyes to understand the ideal of pure reason…

Seasons my shrewd sapience to realize the ideal of pure reason and unifies my soul with the cosmos to slow dance with Mrs. Universe - the womb of wisdom, opulence and mystical miracles...

Immediately opens my eavesdropping eyes to realize I comprise inner intrepid insight, brightens my rainbow enlightened heart to beam esteemed star-powered prowess...

Proudly reveals my 'WOW'-ness, broadcasting my internal Taoist to show people I gregariously gleam genius and liveliness by expressing astute, mesmerizing, spiritual sapience - blatantly telling...

My ethereal and earthly worlds that I have let go of all the undesired and un-required with alligator audaciousness as I let God guide open my power of discernment, unleashing my internal insight...

As I authorize and allow Mrs. Universe - the womb of collaborating charisma - unite my undaunted, garden-fresh ingeniousness; tethering...

My entrepreneurial sagacious spirit, heart, DNA cells, offer me the highest conscious scenery and subconscious landscape to electrify my guts...

To communicate, I expand my stand, unbridling my enterprising exalting astuteness, natural-'eyes'-zing the declarations I speak about what I experience as I experience exalting epiphanies…

Accelerating my life experiences, mirroring the roadrunner "BEEP, BEEP;" triumphantly telling the universe diverse, prosperous sagacity electrifying my defying gravity…

With gyrating revolutionary acuity, I vivaciously incite my Yule-Tide pride to meekly thrive in face of forthright challenges because I instantly recognize my challenges…

As enterprising energies; unmasking my emotional effrontery vanguard 'pard' to peerlessly parade auspicious regal daringness to confess I profess my preeminent, robust, omnificent feistiness…

And express suave, sassy percipience - unlocking my strutting 'savant' cockiness with an idyllic idolization that unmasks my miracle- 'eyes'-zing magician…

Miraculously unleashing cosmic kinetic cooperation in the universe - stylish synchronization as I artfully articulate awesome audacity to express the fact that…

Here I arise in a hurricane of heroism, as I am amplifying Maharishi Sapience! Here I go riding the universal winds of wealth and the tides of triumph seas to stellar success…

Collaborating clouds and expressing clear love as I open undaunted, devout significance and unveil my gallant, omnipotent, bold electro-dynamic eulogies prospering copiously...

Effervescently enjoying every day by peacefully brighten-'eyes'-zing inflaming epitomes, prodigiously unflinching in my daily experiences to beam my brilliant gallantry to say:

I am on the move!

I am telecasting my groovy, genuine realness by opening omnificent visions - 'YES'-ing my life to yell:

"I can! All People can!"

So together, when I tell people what I am doing to sooth my ego, I am really asking people, God, and Mrs. Universe for permission, because when I pell-mell, my timidity tells that I am *really* searching for security in the outer world rather...

Than showing the world *I* am the soothsayer savant with a free-flowing glow of genuine, lively, omnipotent wisdom. Because in hierophant highness I am opening and discovering new ways...

To show people my sassy hegemony - my omnificent 'whoosh' that flawlessly lets the outer world play its game as I go *inside my wise* to whimsically incite sapient, emotional energy...

To engage newborn omniscience revelations that galvanize my Yahweh epiphanies and my playfulness to unveil "Hail!" to the newborn eulogies within my skin...

As I am the North Star avatar of my entertainer, unleashing proud, loud liveliness that opens the unique Divine - the universe's marquee lights that delight my light of freedom to brighten...

My copious luxury. This shines in my life and showcases my innate love, innovation, freedom epiphanies as I ravishingly radiate winsome wealth and superstar success instantly to eternity...

In the right way...in a loving way...in a gloriously blessed way, under grace in a prosperous, perfect way and in Divine order now...

I Am The Sprightly Light of My Hearts Delight

I am the sprightly light of my hearts delight, dawning and energizing lively innovation by gallantly highlighting, tithing, and lubricating the liberating of my global 'get up and go!'

Expressing my prophet-'eyes'-zing newborn and expanding my wisdom by beaming omnipotent, regal nirvana into the cosmopolitan cosmos...

Opening up rabble-rousing, electrifying genius and livening the invigorating visions. Energizing and inciting

newborn gutsiness that 'unbowed my wow.' Unleashing my 'POW' of the brazen sanguine me in the 'Tao of Now,' freed my creed of wisdom. Oracle-'eye'-zing wealth powerfully opens my willingness. Narrating omniscient wizardry frees my spree to showcase sumptuous prosperity, revving up my enterprising energies...

To paint my robust Rembrandt portrait of who I am and where I am going on my universal canvas, unleashing the 'POW of Tao' within. Unshackling the kudos in my heart...

Unbinding the gallantry of my genuine Gandhi unties the lies of my drama that I have been told by society, the school system, and the stealth controllers...

This releases me to be in the 'flow of the go' by letting go of my ingrained rage to page my visionary sage to engage my sagacious sage...

To "Hail!" hallowed harmony in the gallivanting galaxy by unveiling my triumphant revered audaciousness to LOVE living every day...

To recognize the panorama of the liberation of the worldly 'word,' to expand and understand. I encompass the sassy pizzazz...

To show me that my innermost can see and achieve the worldly vista where I visualize infinite success, tenaciously applauding the omnipotent me. I canonize my abilities - my natural success - because I choose to be in the 'flow of the go,' to live in the glow while glistening liveliness and opening out my winning ways by listening to my intrepid intentions...

Crafting the wraith of my choices by realizing I contain the audacious astuteness to WIN my game of life, and have boldly and brilliantly WON my game of life by following a brightened, enlightened, sunlit path!

I authorized my Inner Shine to flow...to glow in daily escapades in order to feel the sheen of pristine serenity!

I am the sprightly light of my hearts delight!

This Knowledge un-tethers my 'prize of my wise,' unfettering my Yahweh to open the way for my free-flowing sovereignty - health, wealth, wisdom - and galvanizing grandeur to beam the gleam of genius.

As I see my name shining in the marquee lights, I magnificently experience life in lavish avalanches of copious opulence...

Today and every day, in an enriched, free way!

As I sashay down my 'Walk of Fame,' zinging the zeal of my free, ardent, monarch essence in a enhancing, dancing way...and in Divine Order - NOW!

I Applaud My Divine Deity

I applaud my divine deity in snappy, parvenu paradigm to understand that I canonize, aggrandize and naturalize my 'I can' ways...

Sanctifying my curiosity, abounding newborn willingness to let fly my lively wisdom, igniting love and living imaginatively by nurturing genius...

Nimbly energizing my 'superstar' stalwart to engage my inner sage and thrill my visionary by unbinding my core courage and lighting my heart's luminary delight...

To expand my wisdom; to energize my forthright, enterprising valor; and to decree my entrepreneurial zeal!

Thus, freeing my spiritual spree and unbridling a 'Kentucky Derby Winning Wit' to witness innovative thunder that opens people's minds to understand when they set boundaries, cancel a thought, or reject something in their life...

They are ingraining *new* limitations and smearing *new* fears into their subliminal landscape, binding their minds into playing victims...

The 'couch-potato' game of shame which is a fictitious game that has been ingrained for so long it has turned into an awful realness by inner dialog, and listening to the condemnations put forth by others…

And by playing in society's corporate-cloned sham that's put forth to be the patrol of the stealth-control and is only freed by grasping the inner mechanism that unlocks the chill-axing of…

Their pioneering preeminence to be the lionized leader of their Divine deity; to be free in their spiritual spree; to live in the bright light of their Divine white light, to take flight in a sapient 'seventh heaven' way…

As I embellish my intuitive insightfulness I applaud my Divine deity, unlatching my dauntless, invigorating visions and instigating my natural-born, enterprising

'Declaration of Independence.'

This expands and tantalizes my Yahweh to open the way for me to 'soar in my core' - 'to walk my talk' - 'to sunbathe on beaches of brilliant, effusive affluence,' by canonizing my harmonious expansive success as…

I ride wave after wave of cascading cash flow. To be in the 'flow of the glow' of galvanizing gusto…

Today and every day, in a royal, rich way!

I Am Omnific Terrific, Savoring Sassy, Sumptuous Success!

I am omnific terrific, savoring sassy, sumptuous success because I confess I glisten when I listen to my sovereign genius. Gloriously verbal-'eyes'-zing enterprising eulogies from a classy innovator...

Daringly releases true-life innovation from my inner royal kingdom, victoriously beaming grandiose boldness and gleaming phenomenal clarity by showcasing genuine regal rareness...

Unsealing my real 'Omni-oracle,' edifying omnipotence and magnetizing newborn ingenuity by opening a "WIN-a-tude" attitude, fantastically innovating cosmopolitan television and expanding robust riches...

Invigorating freedom and igniting courageous stalwart audacity, visually opening opulent resources and inviting new, galvanizing sapience to authorize my superstar Yahweh...

Suavely unleashing majestic prodigies and tantalizing omnipotent Utopian savvy by subliminally unlocking sanguine sanctity, and thanking my titanium backbone with my whole heart...

I also thank God, Mrs. Universe - the womb of enterprising energy - and all the people in the world for sharing their life-expanding wisdom that they expressed to me, energizing my infinite intelligence...

As the wisdom I expressed expanded their life, allowing them to fly in a new philosophizing way. Together, our wisdom expands the synergizing sapience throughout the cosmos...

To broaden our brilliant rainbow omniscience. So I applaud my discerning entrepreneurial newness in the people that never understood that they encompassed the innovative wit until now...

Willfully invent tangible gadgets that enable people to live easier in every facet of their daily life by unlocking newfound prosperity....

Because my undaunted Titan unsheathed that newborn wisdom that utilized my wise-winning, intra-stellar vigor that abounds in the now open celebration of my 'YEA'-sayer nirvana...

In an astounding way because I choose to let go of society's oppressing ways; because I told my bold identity to be the spry piety of my artful self-expression...

Opening a parvenu way to understand people and encompass insurmountable volumes of vibrant oracle liveliness, unleashing maharishi enlightenment...

As I walk in the light of the pristine illumination of my naturalness, broadcasting my Divine destiny acumen that I attained from stainless stateliness that was poetically polished…

Because I choose to look into my soul, by reading my sublime mind 'book' to let go of the moldy old crap that I now understand created chaos and introduced catastrophes so I could live in drama…

But I energize challenge after challenge because challenges are raw wealth, exalting from my fiery desires, and open the way to expand my wisdom…to unleash my enterprising energies…

Unlocking my liberating writer to scribe bright new passages in my subliminal pathways, opening my conscious mind to expand my visionary veracity…

Opening the way for my lively, luxurious worthiness to glow from my heart as glow flows into the universal ethers, effortlessly freeing love and energizing the worldly wealth for others…

This authorizes my opalescent opulence to flow to me in bold bountiful ways, electrifying, galvanizing, and unleashing my cascading cash flow stemming from a wealth of money making ideas…

Thus, I walk down my profound 'Hall of Fame'
corridor fathoming the experience of my
'Buckingham Palace Prosperity,'

Today and every day, in a plush, lush way.

I Am a Spiritual 'Seer' Energizing My Omniscient Omnificence!

I am spiritual 'seer' energizing my omniscient omnificence. To clearly see my all-wise, innovative inventor, electrifies my savvy sagacity...

Boldly transforming my: "I told you so 'get-up and go'" into quick action.

Ignites my kick-ass, sassy audacity and unseals my wheeler-dealer luminary visionary, unleashing my Divine designer ad brilliantly brightening my bona fide oracle wit...

In my core décor introduces and produces my keen, forthright, imaginative force to catch fire in my innermost dauntless desires, initiating the appreciation of my 'omnific, terrific, ingenious artistry'...

To expand people's lives by expanding my *kingdom of wisdom*, allowing them to experience a life filled with lively, intuitive freedom...

Enabling their all-wise, unrestrained, innovative power energizes their philosophizing, pioneering 'seer' to open out their peerless, prosper-'eyes'-zing prophecies to realize a preferred life in a picture perfect way…

Opening the way for people to 'treasure the pleasure' in engaging in their inspired spiritual journey, inaugurates their magical enlightenment…

Allowing people to let go of their meager uneager fears. Freeing their unconquerable soldier and unbridling their triumphant Titan clears their pathways in a brazen bold way…

As I listen boldly to my newborn soothsayer 'YEA'-sayer to walk into my land of clouds incognita, loudly galvanizes my soldier of fortune who will be setting free…

My gloriousness. I explore my moxie to soar through the door by opening my land of clouds incognita, where my parvenu acuity waits patiently for me to arrive in order to thrive in my dreamland cognitions…

Broadening my brilliant brainpower opens the way for the universe to shower me with my well-deserved, lavish avalanches of sumptuous abundance…

As I grasp the candidness of my prestigious-ness, showcasing the upshots of my judicious accomplishments, because I encompass potentate clout to walk into the stormy clouds of chaos with my visions, to ride the tide of my optimum opulence…

Enjoying my 'cloud nine' frills and the thrilling realness of cognizing the dreamland extravaganza of my never-ending overflow of lavish avalanches of sumptuous abundances…

"Whoop-de-doing" the fun dance in the sun, sashaying down my 'Walk of Fame' for high pay in a wonderful way…

Today and every day, in a picture perfect way.

Planting the seeds of my dignified deeds and real-'eyes'-ing my entrepreneurial acumen magnetizes my resourceful revelations to unlock the cockiness of the inventive ingenuity with real brainy *new-i-t-y…*

Unbinding my mind to grasp the sapience, I tantalize my 'YEA'-sayer prayers to innovate, motivate, and invent my way to success with my omnipotent oracle openness and highlighting my delightful heart acuity by branding my life with marquee prosperity…

To incite and excite my cascading cash flow from my inner inventor because I now understand that I encompass the astounding, abounding percipience - harmonizing omniscient omnificence, prosper-'eyes'-zing genuine genius to empower my life...

Because *I am the man with winning plan*, realizing I am the 'prize of my wise' to relish in the triumph of independence by letting go of 'thinking' money comes from a company, corporation, or an outside source...

Opens out a new shrewd understanding that *I am the source of my supply*, opening otherworldly resources, cultivating my instinctive avant-garde innovator to experience...

My life with rousing enthusiasm, authoring my fortune accounts to swell from my prosperity flows in the glow of gigantic lively opulence. Unleashing my 'WOW'...

Tells the world my wisdom opens up my blazing, amazing love in *all* facets of life, living today in my mountain villa - an unrestrained utopia...

Today and every day, in an omnific, terrific way.

Divine Light

Infinite Spirit opens the way for me to be with the Divine in me, shining my divine light, sunlight bright! Setting free my spiritual spree gives free rein to my savant knight…

To glide with potentate pride across the universal sky, embellishing my hierophant chutzpah, unboggles my conscious mentality and spurs on my suave clairvoyant…

My full-throttle mettle unwinds my Divine, sublime mind which unfetters my undaunted, utopian, supercharged, diesel determination. This unlocks…

My cocky, enterprising, emotional engine to declare:

I am rare!

Daring my innate sapience to energize my lively, intrepid love…

To live out loud, vibrating exuberance, I find myself on a scampering rant, unbridling my parlancing, rabble-rousing, raving wit to wave to all the prospering people in a brave new way…

To show that my gallivanting gallantness gleams; it glimmers golden and glamorous, allowing luxury and amazing the ecosphere with forthright 'founding father' sovereignty...

Revolution-'eye'-zing the ethereal endears acumen-'eyes'-zing over-the-top, regal liveliness by declaring I play in my "Wonderful World of Free-Flowing Wealth" today, as I claim my financial fame...

Wisely winning every day, aggrandizing my influential affluence to do what I choose to do in my festive feistiness, to broadcast my wild, unquestionable, unconquerable risk...

Because I choose to cut loose from the mundane inflammation created by the 'follow the herd' transformation that shoved corporate-cloning, college-medication down my throat...

From sheep/people education that hypocritically invoked and poked my conscious mind making me feel stone cold and sold out with doubt, to pitifully pout...

Like I was eating oxy-*cotton*, reeling in a repetitive, sedative loll of being cloned in corporeal competition distantly twisted me in distrust...bent me over in 'dolt!' oldness...

Sent me into a silly stupor that is now gone like the mule train when I opened my eyes to my soul and my soul opened my eyes to see...

I was the one wallowing in the 'follow' mentality because I tried to live the lily-livered lie in order to fit in to the societal 'humdrum' medication that left me crying in my lifeless beer with a sneering fear…

Because I was wallowing in my ridiculous 'head-up-my-rear,' dead-end road…drinking the unchangeable pain. To change my thoughts, to change my life was necessary…seeing as that the 'Kool-Aid' left me feeling dreadfully…

Dead-ended in the hood leaving my dreams homeless because I felt good in my conscious mind, while my subconscious lewdly laid around braiding the same old 'rope-a-dope' myopic beliefs and employing the same epic faith which are the thieves of my dreams…

Casting me off into mundane disdain of how I wished I would have listened instead of blowing blistering lies, ostracizing and wilting in negativity 'golly-gee' I wish I was someone else…as I wake in the same 'fake-and-bake' mindset.

Today is NOW! Awesomely released and amazingly let me go into heavenly bliss, as I climbed into the cockpit of my trendsetting Mars lunar rocket of liberation…

To fly away as a superstar avatar, telling the biosphere I am a winner, televising my worthiness and igniting newborn nirvana by enticing…

My rabble-rousing grit. I get to disavow giving a 'hoot' about society's pouting doubt and jeering, searing jealousy...

Because I honorably 'toot my own horn' loudly, undoes my laudable lore and broadcasts my tenacious, owlish omnipotent, tantalizing enterprising-wise...

In the eyes of Mrs. Universe - the womb of my endless torrential money stream - because I choose to glow in the gleaming, lavish, omniscient wisdom - telling the world...

You watch me soar! As I soar, I open my eyes to fly away into my copious cornucopia, telling the world to 'kiss my *life of riley*' at my amusement park while I ride the coaster of my cascading cash...

Dreamboat...I embark and hark to my starlight bright insight, televising all aboard to my 'Galaxy Gala of Gigantic Opulent Richness.' I glamorize and emblazon brazen enlightenment in my heart to smartly say, "I rest in festive, zestful zeal today, because I played to win in my skin and now my electrified imaginative soul shows nothing but opalescent"...

Unrestricted luminosity with a daylight foresight delights me to say:

I won!

I won because I trusted my innate abilities to facilitate my internal mystical magicians...

Instinctive intuition for me to instantly witness the fruition on my intuitive intentions, as I now play in a nuance of lavish, lively, luxury - embellishing...

My exalted celebration and catapulting me into a copious cornucopia where I bask in the ultimate utopia...

Today and every day...expanding in every way...

In a heart loving way...in the right way...in a Divine, blessed, pristine, blissful way...

And in serenity, I am me!

Broadway Brilliant
Cowboy Wisdom Visionary Vitality

'Eye' see that I am *Broadway Brilliant*, unleashing my Yahweh - my bearer of enterprising energies - and opening the way for my wealth, wisdom, innovation, love, listening and fortifying...

My emotional acumen by un-tethering forthright, esteemed feelings and un-cluttering my vitalizing ingenious philosophies, vividly visioning that I understand **I can**! I expand avidity...

Freeing my inner mechanism to birth my dreams because birthing gives life to my intuitive innovations, unbinding my innermost, trailblazing, curious zeal...

To explore, expand, and energize enterprise by experiencing the zooming zest of my pioneering spirit to birth my dreams into mature realizations...

So I adamantly choose to birth my dreams! Live my dreams! Experience my dreams...in my everyday life with an animated passion, relishing dignified, rich, effusive abundance...

Marveling inside lavish avalanches of copious copiousness from now to eternity in a enlivened, enlightened way...

Boldly revolution-'eye'-zing omnipotent artistry, describing wealth, appreciating my YHWY birthing regal innovation and listening, loving, intently and audaciously...

Naturalizing triumph by showcasing my *Broadway Brilliant Backbone* to daringly tango in nascent nirvana; unlatching...

A crystal clear, brand new understanding in my core scenery and physical landscape to birth my desired love, wealth and success. This engages my innermost willingness to realize that freedom flows when I instantly let go in this moment...

Forthrightly choosing to forever, always, and in all ways expand out and through the beyond, thinking that there's 'right' and 'wrong' people who are different, and that I lack wisdom because other people have told me that. This 'factual' society is full of encumbrances...

I have been taught to think I know business before people, corporate cloning, poverty consciousness, impoverished DNA, sheep-taught school systems that never say no to gossip...

Broaden all peoples *Broadway Brilliant Daringness*! Enjoy this electrifying proverb!

When I am gossiping at the water cooler I am living a pessimistic life dictated by distrust in my own abilities...

When I *am* the gossip of the water cooler I am experiencing life **my way**; I am fearlessly trusting my abilities in a lively, rich way...

Unshackling this sharp-witted newborn pathway and setting free my pioneering nomadic trailblazer gutsiness to meet...

My dreams, intentions, desires, wealth, success, love, innovation, and more, on a mountain peak overlooking a pristine mountain valley showcasing streams of success...

That ardently flow into my rivers of prosperity; that magnificently meander into my oceans of wealth, watching wave after way of cascading cash flow swell my bank accounts beyond my wildest dreams as...

My sunshine of unconditional love supplies the ethers of the cosmos with idyllic tranquility, opening the way for me to appreciate, receive and accept the universe's gift of free-flowing love...

Unlocking my new-fangled visionary so that I may utili-'eye'-ze the clear blue sky as Picasso visualized his canvas...

My dreams and desires reveal effusive, affluent miracles by unchaining this new-fangled wonderment by tilting my head to the dawning heavens until my right eye and left eye focus on one point in the sagacious sky, authorizing...

My left brain and right brain to be one artistic Rembrandt in my mind's eye, setting free...

My inner landscape to visualize and birth my cherished connection of heart, imagination and innovation, with an outcome that will allow me to experience the profuse profusion in my corporeal world...

By utilizing the sagacious, serene sky as the canvas I send my conscious mind on site liberates my inquisitive artist to birth...

My Picasso of appreciation, love, prosperity and accomplishment in the fertile heavens, as the immaculate blue sky is my canvas...

Unshackles my heartfelt understanding, allowing my freedom to flow when I let go undauntedly and unfasten my *Broadway Brilliant Vivid Imagination* to paint my real life mural of...

My enterprising energies! I understand that **I can** expand plush prosperity codes in the movie screen of my cells, temple, mind, heart, spirit, DNA and soul...

As I walk in the quintessence of my alluring terra incognita, all the while discovering the wisdom, fortitude, and love as I eavesdrop on the wisdom of the cosmos savoring tantalizing love, smelling my oceans of wealth...

Touching my streams of success, hearing the waterfalls of fun, seeing my rivers of prosperity and opening my freedom so that when I let go the flow raises the curtain on my *Broadway Brilliant Show*...

I am the Rembrandt that painted my desired life by emancipating my pioneering sage that birthed my desired life, liberating my Picasso to appreciate my fame and fortune...

In a Broadway Brilliant Way!

Animated Adroit Wit

Infinite Spirit, I give thanks for my YHWY opening the way for animated adroit wit to expand my innovation, energizing my enterprising entrepreneur...

To experience my pristine destiny of my plush pleasures on cloud nine, understanding I experience heaven on earth in...

My core landscape, authorizing my soul to beam with stainless luminary brilliance, revealing...

My YHWY is my 'God Eternal' aligning my vision, emotions, thoughts and feelings to make up my forthright sovereign-'I'-zing aura...

To, frankly, focus on minding my affairs and realizing that what I say about somebody or something is me really talking about **me**, therefore when I see wealth and success in others...

I am instigating lavish avalanches of affluent abundances on myself, as I idyllically lie in a feather bed of billion dollar bills in a wealthy winning way...

Opening out an enlivened, enriched paradigm that 'God is my Genius,' optimizing daring, emotional energies and relishing my spiritual sapience...

To engage in my daily encounters by mirroring the three ways that YHWY energizes the world text, numbers, and communication by unlocking a new way of living life in the moment...

Freeing me to understand my DNA is my emotional energy unleashing my sunny charisma and setting free my forthright feelings. That I am worthy and deserving...

To live in lavish luxury with me realizing that luxury is living affluently and vivaciously in seventh heaven; loving universal-'eye'-zing X-ray utopia; revolution-'eye'-zing rabble-rousing...

Thoughts and unleashing my enterprising genius to manifest never-ending, copious, cascading cash flow into all my accounts...

Sending me on an ingenious experience, relishing my spiritual way of life, sanctioning me to recognize the gravity of the earth as the ethers of the universe unbridle...

A snappy savant sagaciousness by blasting off my megastar, superstar quintessence and magnetizing the ethers of the galaxy. Wisdom, innovation, love and laughter manifests...

All my posh desires to sail on my cosmic yacht of luxurious cornucopia in a prolific, prophet-singing way.

My Tangy Sprightliness Zeniths My Inspiring Clarity

My tangy sprightliness zeniths my inspiring clarity and lights up my pure, clear visions of my plucky purposes by painting a panoramic portrait of pristine prosperity on every horizon; opening my mind's eye...

To theater-'eyes' the birthing and experiencing of my sired desires in the 'flow of the go;' my shiny stainless preeminence revealing my tangy sprightliness that zeniths my inspiring clarity, purposefully initiating quantum universal abundance...

Naturally tantalizing my passion and expanding robust kingship by igniting my enterprising superstar, sagaciousness harmonizing, my intuitive gutsiness, hallowing thaumaturgy, illuminating newborn genius...

Magnificently 'YES'-ing my love life, audaciously unlocking dauntless acumen and brilliantly letting go as I energize lithe utopian credence and internally declare my innovative tenacity; 'YAH'-zing...

My daily adventures to indenture my regal, rich, entrepreneurial talent to tenaciously and ardently live every day in a new way -

triumphantly expanding my wisdom; energizing…

My innovative landscape; electrifying my enterprising euphoria; galvanizing effusive epiphanies while eagerly looking into the eyes of my daily life and asking this question…

How is this event the greatest life-expanding event that ever emerged in my daily scenery? How does this purge the 'whoop-de-do' drama of my daily escapades by eliminating…

The dormant torment of trauma in my core conspirator to suavely surge in courageous curiosity by igniting my light of life, galvanizing my genius, opening the way for…

My winds of wisdom to blow? I feel my breezes of brilliance enter my prospecting prophecies to magnanimously magnify the embellishing and relishing of every event, real-'eye'-zing…

My life is a jubilee of jovial utopia, brightly illuminating enticing, effervescent rainbows to soar across the heavens, real-'eye'-zing I am the pot of gold at the end of…

My own rainbow. I colorfully express who I am in a peerless 'seer' way to glow in the glide of **who I am**; to ride the universal vista in a superstar avatar way…

Today and every day…

As I sail the ocean blue in bountiful luxury, unleashing common sense foresight in an unembarrassed way to lavishly cherish...

My unlimited overflow of wealth, wisdom and friendship in every facet of my life, broadening the charismatic colors in the worldly scenery and opening the way for...

Me to see, feel, smell, taste and touch my cascading opulent opulence that fills all my prosperity accounts in the...

WOW of the POW, NOW! in a rich, lively way!

My Spiritual Star Unsheathes My Worldly Wisdom

My spiritual star unsheathes my worldly wisdom to understand the panorama of expansion by unlatching the gate of attachment, unbinding my inner scenery...

To see the world as a sashaying swashbuckler, suavely expanding my enterprising endeavors and freeing my daring visionary sage...

To view the universal landscape as a preeminent adventurer, nobly opening rich, adamant, millionaire astuteness to ravishingly enhance the prance of...

Pristine, robust, acute nirvana - correlating expansive, panoramic omnipotence - and unlashing my canonized cascading cash flow to sumptuously stream into...

My ever-growing prosperity account, unhinging the synergy of 'snazzy jazzy' worldly wisdom, wowing opulence, revolution-'eye'-zing rabble-rousing, love decreeing, lively 'YES'-es...

Winning instantly, sanctifying dauntless, omniscient magnificence that authorizes my inner me to be free to express...

My feisty fervent acuity by undoing my annuity; actualizing newborn nirvana and unleashing my intuitive thaumaturgy as Yahweh allows me...

To dance the 'flashdance' of triumph to chime the rhyme of sumptuous success in my subliminal mind; to unleash my spiritual star, unsheathing my world wisdom...

To recognize the 'prime time wise' in the panorama of expand - out through and into the parvenu paradigm of pristine prosperity. I choose to wisely reside inside...

In a gliding great way...

Today and every day, taking a rich regal ride on the Reading Railroad way...

I Pass 'go,' collecting my billionaire bounty in a rich, preeminent way.

My Mind Is Clear and My Visions Are Pure

My mind is clear and my visions are pure. My heart is light, like the fuse on the Fourth of July Fireworks in Central Park as I glide into the 'flashdance'...

To unwind the bind of my undaunted newborn wisdom, opening-out, never-ending, dazzling discernment; applauding my zooming zeal and living in-the-moment by naturally globetrotting and expressing...

My enterprising 'wise,' waking innovative sapience in every body to free the world spree, opening the way for sumptuous prosperity-to-be-realized by everything and everybody...

Because folks untree'd their need for greed and buried the taunt of want by unshackling the lack in their poverty consciousness to clear their mind, freeing the mind's eye and allowing their visions to be pure...

Undoing their 'woo-woo,' introducing the producing pioneering sprightliness to light the bright in their omniscience essence, unleashing the kapish of...

Their opportunistic landscape, kinetically galvanizing their intuitive scenery; unlocking the locks of their innovative inventions; expanding the universal landscape…

To experience life in a easier, effortless way as they unbound their wound-up, egotistical haughtiness to see the sassy, sapiential spree, allowing them…

To be 'themselves' by unwinding their mind, untying the strings of yesterday's 'show glow' of their genuine liveliness, optimizing wisdom to be the gallivanting savant in their daily life…

Opening out their canonized cascading cash flow as I play on my 'beaches of bountiful,' expanding affluence and correlating harmony by energizing sassy success in every facet of…

My life, living by surfing wave after wave of wealth…

Today and every day, in cherished ways, and in Divine order…<u>NOW</u>!

Wisdom Illuminations

My wisdom illuminations highlight my idolized abilities to ride the tides of my sassy superstar savvy; to bust the rust on my ingrained pain of the mundane money game...

Unlocking a self-assured cockiness to walk my talk of wisdom, activating love and kindling omnipotent freedom, tantalizing adroit knight-errantry, kinetically energizing...

The universal ethers with canonized clarity. I gallantly soar in roaring robust opulence, applauding acumen-'eye'-zing, revolutionizing innovation, galvanizing my never-ending flow of lavish avalanches of affluent abundances...

Today and every day, in a laudable 'applaud'-able way!

As I am gleaming esteemed, preeminent prosperity from my heart in the right way, in a loving way under grace, in a Divine blessed way, and in glowing Divine order, <u>NOW</u>!

Electrifying Oomph

'Eye' am electrifying oomph, sending forth a powerhouse of sapient sassiness and jolting the universe with high-voltage vividness by lighting up folk's desires, passions and purposes...

Just like the lights on the Las Vegas Strip on New Year's Eve, as I experience and enjoy illuminated, plush copiousness as my sassy savvy KO's the gloom in the universe...

Lighting a fire in people's 'grit and go to,' allows them to experience jovial jubilees, expressing their oracle opulence as I bask in wealthy wittiness...

Enjoying my powerhouse of prosperity energizes my daily emancipation that sets me free in my spiritual abundance under grace, in nova newness instantly to infinity...

Golden New Way

'Eye' open my listening prowess to see a golden new way to experience my love, innovation and freedom – energizing my savvy utopia to step into my enterprising endeavors...

Unleashing genuine omnipotent leadership dexterity by engaging a new-way to expand wisdom, wealth, and acuity; 'YAH!'zing jazzing...

My Yahweh to open the way for my clear-sightedness. I understand I can expand moxie by setting free my listening prowess to hear my winning wisdom that I daringly wrote...

In my declaration of my sovereign-'eye'-zing wealth, innovation, love and laughter, I choose to experience my pristine, prosperous 'Heaven on Earth' journey...

I ardently express in my metaphysical and physical legacy theater-'eye'-zing my vivid visions in my mind's eye by energizing my emotional sagaciousness; vitalizing...

my forthright feelings to audaciously realize I trust my abilities, galvanizing my genius to blatantly engage in my journey into my terra incognita understanding...

My undaunted, newborn determination enlightens robust stamina, trusting adroit, nascent, Divine innovation; nobly generating a lavish cascading cash flow, enriching my life...

Authorizes me to encourage, enlighten, enrich, enhance, energize, and emancipate – expansively expand folks into wealth and success by unbolting their wisdom, innovation, love, listening and prodigies...

To hear their whispering wisdom and trusting in their abilities to communicate in the moment to love who they are and where they are going; this allows them to love everything and everybody in the universe…

Real-'eyes'-ing the universe – everything and everybody – loves them in a lively, enlivened way; opening the way for the populace of the world, including me, to understand…

By fissuring their paradoxes that are hidden in their subliminal DNA physical landscapes, unhooking their human plow of ingrained poverty, waiting for somebody else…

To do everything for us thinking that the political arena is my best interest at heart; corporate fascism cloning life is about business, and business before people, egotistical priggishness…

Because life is a people business and people 'talking' to people and business is nothing more than a name on a document for tax identification and branding, etc…

Unfastens this new paradigm that All People and I totally understand: I never talk to a business or businesses, I talk to people inside the business which unlocks this golden new way…

To experiencing life with gusto, genius, and being able to understand success tantalizing opulent opulence and freeing my inner mechanism to recognize since the beginning of time that life…

Has consisted of text communication and numbers with every living organism consisting of hydrogen, oxygen, carbon and nitrogen. Therefore, we are brought forth...

On this journey as energy conceived in an energizing act; we live in energy, unlatching this premise that 'I am' enterprising energy, unleashing my spiritual sapience to see the universe...

As seeds of wisdom expanding into sequoias of sapience, emancipating my heart heartiness, unleashing my innovative élans, unshackling my entrepreneurial endeavors, freeing...

My undaunted utopian to foxtrot with my desire of profuse profusion...in a lavishly rich way...as I ride the Pennsylvania Railroad to Boardwalk, collecting my $10,000,000 of Divine inheritance...

As I 'Pass Go,' galvanizing omnipotence and singing on Broadway my songs of innovation, expressing my 'Master of Ceremonies' sumptuous success...

Unlatching the flood gates on my waterfall of lavish avalanches of copious abundances as I dance the tango of tranquility, listening to my winds of wisdom optimizing...

Emmy award-winning wealth and freeing me to send out unconditional love to receive and accept unconditional love in a wealthier, healthier way...

I Am Sunrise Wise Revealing My Sunset Supremacy

I am sunrise wise revealing my sunset supremacy, soaring through the instinctual cosmos at an avatar altitude, televising my stainless aptitude, broadcasting my Thor attitude...

To smile in the eye of a challenge while I laugh in the face of chaos, realizing I am encompassing the 'rock-em, sock-em, knock-em' galvanizing grit 'get up and go'...

To expand my imaginative wisdom; to unbind my mind; to wind up my sagacious magnanimous intuitive love, expanding throughout and beyond every challenging dare...

That is innate to my purposeful journey because Mrs. Universe - the womb of enterprising energies - my intentions and God, purposefully, passionately and lovingly place in...

My path. Planting astute, tantalizing, home-grown honor, ethics and morals as the code of real respect I have for myself in my innermost landscape. Therefore, I set free...

My commitment, optimistic discernment and engage my innermost, courageous curio by expanding my sapience and energizing my 'enterprising wise'…

To savor every experience I flamboyantly encounter with galvanizing gusto, because I optimistically understand that a challenge and chaos are the letting go of moldy old, stuck-in-the-mud attachments…

To yesterday's ways. This knowledge opens my spirit, heart, mind and temple, unlocking my forthright fortitude to look into the eye of chaos' boss, telling the chaos that I see the light of wisdom All People encompass because…

I understand chaos is correlating my highest outcomes, sensationally freeing my inner Christopher Columbus to explore…

My internal savvy philosopher, exposing my winning wherewithal by whimsically harmonizing and edifying robust energized wisdom, igniting tenacious hegemony. Ardently loving my day…

Opens the way for me to walk fancy-free down my affluent avenues of profuse prosperity, because I choose to engage in my heart's journey to be the teacher of my journey…

Because I am the 'buzz of my cuz' - of my opulent optimizing - my 'I can,' attitude is unleashed, zinging zeal and recognizing my zealous Zen buzzes with colorful charisma and honey bee wisdom…

Pollinates my charismatic cosmos with optimistic sovereign solvency, exposing my newborn innovation, unlocking peoples' souls to express their 'I can' fortitude…

Today and every day, in regal rich way…

As I sashay in my heyday of opulent opulence and triumphant terrific-ness in a wise, enterprising way!

My Heart's Delight

I am the sprightly light of my heart's delight dawning, energizing my lively innovation, gallantly highlighting, tithing and lubricating the liberating of my global 'get up and go'…

Expressing my prophet-'eye'-zing newborn wisdom and beaming omnipotent regal nirvana into the cosmopolitan cosmos…

Opening out rabble-rousing, electrifying genius - livening lithe, invigorating visions, inciting…

Newborn gutsiness that unbowed my 'WOW,' unleashing the 'POW' of my brazen sanguine me in the 'Tao of Now,' freed my creed of wisdom…

Narrating omniscient wizardry freed my spree to showcase sumptuous prosperity, revving-up my enterprising energies…

To paint my robust Rembrandt portrait of who I am and where I am going on my universal canvas, unleashing the 'POW of Tao' within and unshackling the kudos in my heart…

Buddha unbinding the gallantry of my genuine Gandhi unties the lies of my drama, all that I have been told by society, the school system, and the stealth control…

47

Releases me to be in the 'flow of the go' of letting go my ingrained rage to page my visionary sage, to engage my sagacious sage…

To hale hallowed harmony in the gallivanting galaxy, unveiling my triumphantly revered audaciousness to love living every day…

To recognize the panorama of the liberation of the worldly word, expand to understand that I encompass the sassy pizzazz…

To show me my innermost 'I can!' by showing the worldly vista where I visualize infinite success, tenaciously applauding the omnipotent me that

I canonize my abilities, naturalizing success because I choose to be in the 'flow of the go'…to live in the glow…glistening liveliness and opening out my winning by listening to my intrepid intentions…

Crafting the wraith of my choices by realizing I contain the audacious astuteness to win my game of life, and have boldly and brilliantly won my game of life in a bright, enlightened, sunlit path…

Because I authorized my Inner Shine to flow…to glow in daily escapades and to feel my sheen of pristine serenity. I am the sprightly light of my heart's delight…

Un-tethers the 'prize of my wise,' unfettering my Yahweh to open the way for my free-flowing sovereignty, health, wealth, wisdom and galvanizing grandeur to beam the gleam of genius as…

I see my name shining in the marquee lights - as I magnificently experience life in lavish avalanches of copious opulence…

Today and every day, in an enriched, enlightened, free way!

As I sashay down my 'Walk of Fame,' zinging the zeal of my free, ardent, monarchial essence in a enhancing, dancing way, and in Divine Order…<u>NOW</u>!

Rainbow Realness

Cowboy Wisdom Visionary Vitality

Thus...I begin...

My colorful astuteness paints *rainbow realness* is the brightness in the stars shining in the universal skies, sparkling with my superstar-avatar, tantalizing audaciousness, revolutionizing sagacity, electrifying...

The solar system with my kaleidoscope of kinetic wisdom; willfully invigorating discernment, optimizing megastar manifestations, broadcasting my brilliant robust omniscience and applauding my...

Dignified credence. All of this greatness allows me to astutely speak the truth, 'igniting-the-lighting' of a new-fangled genius that entices my writing 'wise' to witness my parvenu novelty, naturally opening my visual...

Enterprising lithe, tenaciously 'YES'-ing my profound, unique, glorified, galvanizing wit to open the door to explore my spiritual lore of my inner admirer. To understand that...

Life gets in the way of life, opens the way for me to live in *rainbow realness*, expanding by enterprising wiliness to eternally recognize...

My internal 'prime-time wise' intuition, luxuriously initiating nirvana and embellishing in sumptuous splendor in the magical movie...

Opening the real appeal to my sired desires in my mind's eye; theater-'eye'-zing my solar stellar tango, enhancing the prancing of the 'cash-dance' for people to relish in their colorful charismatic painting...

Their *rainbow realness* is the universal vista, as they sashay through life in a real, robust way; to feel free in the inner spree by understanding life is...

A dance of pristine parvenu, dawning affluence by naturally crafting ever-flowing wealth, winning every day by awesomely loving TODAY!

Having fun in the sun, today and every day, in a rich milk chocolate way!

Opening my 'flash dance of forever,' loving my awesome stalwart honor by declaring amazing newborn coolness and edifying the fact that it is COOL to be the self-ruler of my Divine destiny...

To unleash the polish of preeminent omnipotence, livening-up innovative

supremacy, harmonizing the birthing of my
sired desires...

To fly high in my daily life; to live in the lyrics
of the limelight of my supreme supremacy, of
who I am when I look in my mirror,
mesmerizing the cosmos with my...

Visions of enjoying my canonized cash-dance
on the 'Broadway Stage,' expanding my sunlit
brilliant flamboyancy in a lively lithe way...

***Today and every day, in a free-flowing spree of
Divine order!***

Beaming my gleaming genuine love, energizing
my acumen - mesmerizing and inspiring my
newborn 'get up and go,' expanding...

The 'WOW of the POW-MOW,' opening out
my wisdom, optimizing my wealth and
prosperity - winning today and every day by
unlocking white light innovation in other folks;
unleashing...

Their lightning bolt wisdom to expand their
sand to understand that *they* encompass
canonized abilities to naturalize their lavish
luxury...

Today and every day, in a picture perfect way!

As I sashay down my beaches of bountiful
abundances in a pure, clear, perfect way!

My Colorful Charisma

My colorful charisma televises my 'candid-camera' candor, bestowing my core regal credence to the world as I speak in silence, live in the space of my imaginative imagery, innately expressed...

By my unconquerable clear-cut, shark-quick actions. This emancipates my unquestionable visionary vitality, while my soul's vibrant vulnerability unlocks worldly opportunities, profoundly eulogizing...

My natural 'supreme gunfighter chi' - my 'Herculean strength, potentate wisdom, heart's love, and fearless avant-gardism' - I serve mankind with inspired, sapient, majestic sagacity...

I set free infinite supplies of 'moneyed-up' moxie to enliven the cosmos, cooperating the community with blessed, blissful, innate unity...

To realize that silence is the parlance to the 'flash dance' of pristine, plush prosperity - because money unhampers, dashing miraculous, omnificent, newborn enthusiasm...

Saying 'YES!' to my hell-raising, over-the-top, well-heeled experiences in *all* my daily escapades with sassy, sexy, global-trendsetting enlightenment, let's fly my zealous exuberance…

Realizing money flows to those who unleash their innovative wit into the universe - to win with entrepreneurial cleverness in others that choose to engage and…

Excite their 'get up and go;' to magnify and intensify their wisdom, wealth, health, and new Divine grandeur to play in the NOW with newborn WOW - televising their fresh ideal axioms…

For people to say: "Being the star of my 'candid camera' extravaganza exposes an abounding philosophical rock-n-roll star flair."

Gives a thrill-seeking, free rein to their rollicking, rich and rebellious resume. Allowing them to flow in a fervent, frisky, free way, sends them into frolicking financial freedom and in Divine order…NOW!

As I propel headlong into my adventurous activities, my titanium backbone portrays noble gallantry in order to walk among the people with a mature, quick-witted, forthright fortitude…

Showing people a new 'grand way to play' allows my auspicious actions to become my spoken words as I saunter through life in silence. I unravel my brand new courtly boldness…

To show the world my silence postures my sterling silver quintessence and splendidly serves my sumptuous 'Shangri-La' suaveness. To spin the world like a top articulates…

My phenomenal cosmic chutzpah and unchains my amazing, dauntless, dapper inciter to shamelessly ascend into my mind-blowing, astro-galactic heavens…

As I am a liberated visionary, I authorize and allow me to appreciate embellishing in silence in my daily encounters with my internal landscape patient, and remain unflappable in saucy situations…

Because my silence is my internal peerless valor, endearing me to ensue, appreciate and embrace my parvenu, prudent, prodigious prowess that…

Unleashes inherent artistic pictures in my subliminal scenery to feel, touch, taste, see, smell, listen…and hear.

My inner 'seer' philosopher softly say's in a loud, proud voice, the right pathway for me as my inner soothsayer carries a brilliant bold stick of sapience. Then…I see my universal spree…

In a daring declaration of inspiration, I say, "I am here to play. Embracing my salient prayers of peace and prosperity, displays my gallivanting grandeur in a calm, cool, classy way."

To spearhead the world's wisdom, epitomizing my sapient silence broadcasts that I am the Divine debonair - with an exalting zillionaire zeal that brightens the sky...

With my enlightened mightiness *I am the star*, showing the world my brilliant Oscar that is boldly set on MY mantle of wealth and success as I played, watched, and embellished...

My Emmy award-winning performance, engages me in my daily life's movie because I encompass the guts to live my dreams in silence and walk in the gap of my adroit actions...

Telecast the brash brassiness of the luminary light of my Divine wherewithal as I vehemently voice my daily life jubilee through my visions to hypnotize my opulent, impressive camaraderie...

In my mind's eye, my visions are a majestic mural painted on the horizon - with my tongue being my zealous 'Zorro' that cuts away the lies of my busy, egotistical mind, authorizing me...

To be serene and keen in my utopist spirit. This tells the world my super-luminary prowess and ignites my rabble-rousing imagination; tenaciously invigorating an astronomical speed of prodigious prodigy...

All extols my high-rolling robustness to express my audacious, clear-sighted acuity in silence...*like a lover*...articulating my sheen insightfulness through only the language of my body...

With my eyes full of newborn prophesizing-wise, I heroically hallow my poised effrontery essence in the universal sky, high-fiving...

My champion desires to unleash my financial fire in order to wire the electronic transfer of my mesmerizing wisdom to the universal vista...

As Mrs. Universe - the womb of endless, lavish financial freedom direct deposit's a plush, never-ending cash flow into my prosperity accounts...

As I open my heart in silence - as my heart speaks in neonatal innovation - I announce to the cosmos community that I live my opulent extravaganza in quaint quietness...

I sanguinely lead the world with ingenious wisdom for the ages, as I lay in my hammock between two palm trees, enjoying my bountiful breezes...

Loyalty aggrandizes my peerless stillness as I relish in my inexhaustible copiousness...

Today and every day, in every way, under grace!

In a silky, soothing way…and in calm, pristine, Divine order…NOW!

Immaculate Imagination

My light of 'immaculate imagination' invigorates my mystical magician and showers me with miracles - now to eternity - allowing me to whirl in wisdom from amplified intuition by revving-up my luminary wit...

To whimsically walk in illuminated acumen. Aggrandizing love kinetically tantalizes my Divine light; articulating intrepid insight authorizes me to take my fervent flight to delight the world...

With winsome harmony - igniting real love to flow from my heart to smarten people up so they may see their terrific talents dance across their minds' eye...to instantly 'flash dance' on stage...

On their Broadway show of life, as I star in my African Safari - driving my Ferrari across the Kilimanjaro Valley - with my eyes on the prosperous prize just waiting on the top of my money mountain...

Uncovering and discovering my 'Fountain of Youth' allows me to brashly boogey naked in my dreams, drinking 'nirvana' energy drinks and unveiling...

My earth-shattering, rabble-rousing synergy. Naturalizing a blaze-zing, keen, edifying discernment, extravagantly explodes my bountiful bonfire of desires...

To daringly electrify my soothsayer imagination, energizing my superstar savant to see afar - realizing that affluence frees avatar realizations, sending savvy avant-garde sensations...

Through my heart, soul, spirit, DNA cells, body and mind - winding my chakras up like a Nolan Ryan fastball - rocketing me into an omnificent, omniscient gleam. Unmasking...

My esteemed, immaculate imagination enthralls my unworldly utopia and allows me to be THE earthly energy to excite and ignite people...

To see their talent accelerate and exhilarate their dreams to fruition, instantly unlashing their frolicking, astronomical affluence. Opening people's eyes allows them...

To be the intrepid influencer of their life, rather than hear a sneering jeer from the world as people tear down one another just to give their own egos a ride in pride on the 'pity me' train...

To be restrained in mundane mockery of society, now de-funk and debunk the belief that "I, and the money I make, is gone like Enron"...

Just like Enron was a 'me' cover-up of their own dishonesty, I now understand lies never die, as I realize the story grows until the truth comes through the clouds - radiating like the sun...

On a cloudy day, lies linger in the subconscious mind, but recognizing that the truth can be told in less than seven words - as a lie is told in tiers of tumult - leaving the liar doing summersaults in silliness...

To twist in the wind of time with the rope getting tighter, creating an inner fight, changing into a foolish fighter firing up their naysayer interior dialog...

Until a liar becomes a 'crier,' hemorrhaging in humility and exuding the guts to 'let go' - expanding into being accountable and responsible about their situation...

Saying: "Here is the real deal! I am the one who is lying to all!" This sends me into a freefall of distrust and disgust...

I instantly open out a new realization, sensationalizing the inner landscape that the only one I can lie to is myself. Thus, when I lie to the world, I really lie to my own morals, ethics, and valor...

So now I colossal-eyes my omnipotent-wise. This authorizes me to realize my heart is wise in truth, with extrasensory warrior savvy that lights up my effrontery essence...

To brightly glow...televising across the universe my gleaming, beaming love and opening the window to my soul...sanctioning my soul to send out unconditional love...

Now to eternity!

As I realize the 'truth sets me free' to unleash a sunlit wit, allowing my skin to blaze unrestrained, esteemed energy with a sunrise occurring every second of the day...

As I have opened my eyes to realize that when somebody lies about me they are showing me their dark energy, which shows me they are a jealous jerk and full of foolish envy...

Their darkness awesomely engages the world to listen to *Cowboy Wisdom Innovation Coaching* as *Cowboy Wisdom Visionary Vitality* will set them free in their inner spree to fly like a hummingbird...

To walk with the moxie of a lion; the heart of a Kentucky Derby Winner; the love of a single white dove, as the liars remain twisting in the wind...forever and always blundering in wonder...

When the curtain drops on a liar they are sent into a never-ending spiral downward, as their decisions cause never-ending strife with lies being the robber baron of their dreams…

As I now realize, I live down to a lie. But in truth, I soar like a Bald Eagle to engage in parvenu, escalating insight, energizing emotional enterprising-wise…

To experience life in galvanized gusto; to soar through the universe like a superwoman/superman. When I tell the truth I am the rococo rocketeer in my life, admitting to myself…

I see other people's strength and challenges as grandeur and wisdom - as I am a student with preeminent prudence and I am the 'best in the west,' energizing bold, electrifying sapience; tantalizing…

Infinite newborn astuteness, energizing sassy tenacity in the universal ethers to cut through the lies of liars; to speak an immaculate, imaginative innovation; to spin the universe…

Like a top whistling, winning hegemony instantly by sensationalizing thaumaturgy and igniting newborn genius to flow across the universe like the appearance of a rainbow after a thunderstorm…

With my charismatic wit as sharp as a lightning bolt, I unbolt my guts to walk through the swamp of my terra incognita, because I encompass the collaborating charisma…

64

To expand the worldly landscape with gritty, canonized acumen, opening people's eyes to their inner kingdom of talent...NOW!...in a brazen brash way. As I sing my songs of tantalizing truth...

I cut loose the liars in my life to strive in newness, unleashing my effrontery to the universe. As a stalwart savant to express my egress from allowing people...

To say what they want, understanding my internal desires to light the fire to burn their non-truths instantly, as people see me for who I am - sends the dishonest people in my life on their way...

In very merry, blessed way...to those who lie...shall wither in shame on the inside, blaming the person they lied about for your fall from grace. The disgrace of your lies will never ever die...

As I instantly live in the moment, forthrightly relishing the heaven out of every second of every day because I see my amazing Titan terrific-ness...

I embellish my daredevil talent tango in the light of my cascading cash flow, to relish my vehement voyage by galvanizing my emotional life force as I imprint my maharishi magic...

On the world stage, I express my sagacious sapience to boldly broaden my rainbow wisdom across the worldly landscape, and my life - brashly beautifying the cosmos countryside…

With copious new understanding and innovative insight - I achieve wealth, success, perfect health, love and Divine grandeur - from now to eternity - in a superstar perfect way and in charming Divine order…NOW!

My Mind Is Clear and My Visions Are Pure

My mind is clear and my visions are pure; my heart is light, like the fuse on a 'Fourth of July' firework in Central Park. I glide on to the floor and into the universe to 'flash dance'…

To unwind the bind of my undaunted newborn wisdom, opening-out my never-ending dazzling discernment, applauding my zooming zeal and living in-the-moment - naturally globetrotting and expressing…

My enterprising-wise, waking innovative sapience in every body to free the world spree by opening the way for sumptuous, prosperity-to-be, realized by everything and everybody…

Because folks have un-treed their need for greed and buried the taunt of want, unshackling the lack in their poverty-consciousness to clear their mind, freeing the mind's eye and allowing their visions to be pure…

Undoing their 'woo-woo' and introducing the producing pioneering sprightliness that lights the 'bright' in their omniscience essence, unleashing the kapish of…

Their opportunistic landscape, kinetically galvanizing their intuitive scenery and unlocking the locks of their innovative inventions by expanding the universal landscape…

To experience life in a much easier effortless way, as they unbound their wound-up egotistical haughtiness to see the sassy, sapient spree, allowing them…

To be *them* - unwinding their mind to clear by untying the strings of yesterday's 'show' of their genuine liveliness, optimizing wisdom to be the gallivanting savant in their daily life…

Opening out their canonized cascading cash flow as I play on my 'beaches of bountiful,' expanding my affluence, correlating harmony, energizing sassy success in every facet of my life!

I live by surfing wave after wave of wealth!

Today and every day, in a cherished way, and in Divine order…NOW!

My Visionary Sage

Eye engage my visionary sage to see the world in a wonderful way; to stroll in my Rock-n-Roll Hall of Fame; to be in the 'flow of the go'...

Letting go of yesterday's festering expectations and reality of blistering, lame, mundane, engrained shame; ingraining...

The pain of previous attached instances - nay saying my will to play in the game of my fame - because I choose to listen to the naysayer's, neglecting my savant soothsayer that engaged my inner sage...

So now I choose to impeach the leeches and unchain the virtuous - letting go expansively - experiencing clear, pure, heaven-on-earth, sanguine, pristine prosperity...

I unwind my stainless spine by unlashing my dazzling pizzazz to unshackle my spectacular, liberating libretto; to emphasize my wise; to realize...

Prayer reveals the sex-appeal of omnipotent, serene peace - emancipating my regal integrity and tenaciously 'YES'-ing my Yahweh to open the way for me...

To 'shake, rattle and roll' the worldwide prize of the inner wise in people's hearts and smarts, opening out their hearts delight…

To live their sired desires in a lavish, luxurious experience - in a regal rich way. As I go on my way to sashay down my paved highway of prosperous, acumen-'eye'-zing visions, expanding discernment and harmonizing my innovative genius, hallowing wealth and opulently magnifying the…

Magnanimous, galvanizing newborn ingenuity and freeing my 'YEAH'-zing, intuitive, natural, global, noble preeminence to…

Understand that I encompass undaunted natural determination, energizing real 'stand tall' audacious nobility…

I declare dignity and expand clarity by living astutely and reveling in nimble gracefulness!

To genuinely reveal ardent credence, emblazing flaming unconditional love, nurturing ebullient suave sagacity, I electrify the atmosphere with the pith of NEW-CLEAR, unalloyed prosperity - unlocking robust emolument - authorizing me to reside in…

Enriched, moneyed-up opulence by living ultra-modern-'eye'-zed. Electrifying a new-fangled tour-de-force is my awesome source...

To soar Omni-potently, unleashing real, colossal, enterprising wit to willfully invigorate, tantalizing affluence...

To sunbathe on my beaches of copious utopia, because I engaged my visionary sage to galvanize my opulent outcomes in a dazzling, glamorous way...

Today and every day, in a splendid, supreme way!

Robert A. Wilson

I hope you enjoyed, *Life is Love Innovation Freedom Epiphanies.*. I am Robert Wilson, NLP Practitioner, Clinical Hypnotherapist, Past Regression Specialist, Reiki Master, Radio Show Host, Parts Integration and Time Line Coach.

Cowboy Wisdom NLI Radio is on Tuesday and Thursday at 8PM Eastern/5PM Pacific and has reached out to listeners. Cowboy Wisdom NLI Radio opens people's eyes to see their talent and engage in their intrepid intentions instantly.

Cowboy Wisdom Visionary Vitality opens peoples enterprising listening to unmask your entrepreneurial wise and unleash your canonized abilities so you see all the opulent opportunities to experience your copious outcomes in galvanizing gusto - now to eternity. Cowboy Wisdom Visionary Vitality opens peoples' enterprising eyes with a visionary prowess, authorizing people to live their dreams. Cowboy Wisdom Visionary Vitality expands people's wisdom, energizing their "get up and go"to live their desired life with galvanizing gusto. NLI unlocks people's Neuro Linguistic Innovation from within, authorizing them to see their way to wealth and success. Through rhymes and my life experiences I have uncovered and discovered a way to open the heart with NLI – freeing your innovative intuition to flow into your daily extravaganza.

Robert A. Wilson

www.cowboy-wisdom.com

rob@cowboy-wisdom.com

cwbywsdm@gmail.com

A SPECIAL THANK YOU TO YOU!

On behalf of everyone at Freedom Of Speech Publishing, thank you for choosing Life is Love Innovation Freedom Epiphanies for your reading enjoyment.

As an added bonus and special thank you, for purchasing Life is Love Innovation Freedom Epiphanies, you can enjoy discounts and special promotions on other Freedom of Speech Publishing products. Visit www.freedomeofspeech.com/vip to learn more.

We are committed to providing you with the highest level of customer satisfaction possible. If for any reason you have questions or comments, we are delighted to hear from you. Email us at cs@freedomofspeechpublishing.com or visit our website at:
http://freedomofspeechpublishing.com/contact-us-2/.

If you enjoyed Life is Love Innovation Freedom Epiphanies, visit www.freedomofspeechpublishing.com for a list of similar books or upcoming books.

Again, thank you for your patronage. We look forward to providing you more entertainment in the future.

Life is Love Innovation Freedom Epiphanies
By Robert A. Wilson

For more books like this one, visit Robert A. Wilson's website at:

http://cowboy-wisdom.com/

Printed in the United States of America
The publisher offers discounts on this book when ordered in bulk quantities. For more information, contact Sales Department, Phone 815-290-9605, Email:
sales@FreedomOfSpeechPublishing.com

Freedom of Speech Publishing, Leawood KS, 66224
www.FreedomOfSpeechPublishing.com
ISBN: 1938634144
ISBN-13: 978-1-938634-14-7